Great Earth Science Projects™

Hands-on Projects About
Oceans

Krista West

The Rosen Publishing Group's
PowerKids Press™
New York

Some of the projects in this book were designed for a child to do together with an adult.

Published in 2002 by The Rosen Publishing Group, Inc.
29 East 21st Street, New York, NY 10010

First Edition

Book Design: Michael de Guzman

Photo Credits: p. 4 © PhotoDisc; pp. 6–21 by Cindy Reiman.

West, Krista.
Hands on projects about oceans / Krista West.
    p. cm. — (Great earth science projects)
Includes bibliographical references and index.
ISBN 0-8239-5846-9
1. Oceanography—Experiments—Juvenile literature. [1. Ocean—Experiments. 2. Experiments.] I. Title. II. Series.
GC21.5 .W47 2002
551.46'0078—dc21

                                                                        00-013035

Manufactured in the United States of America

Contents

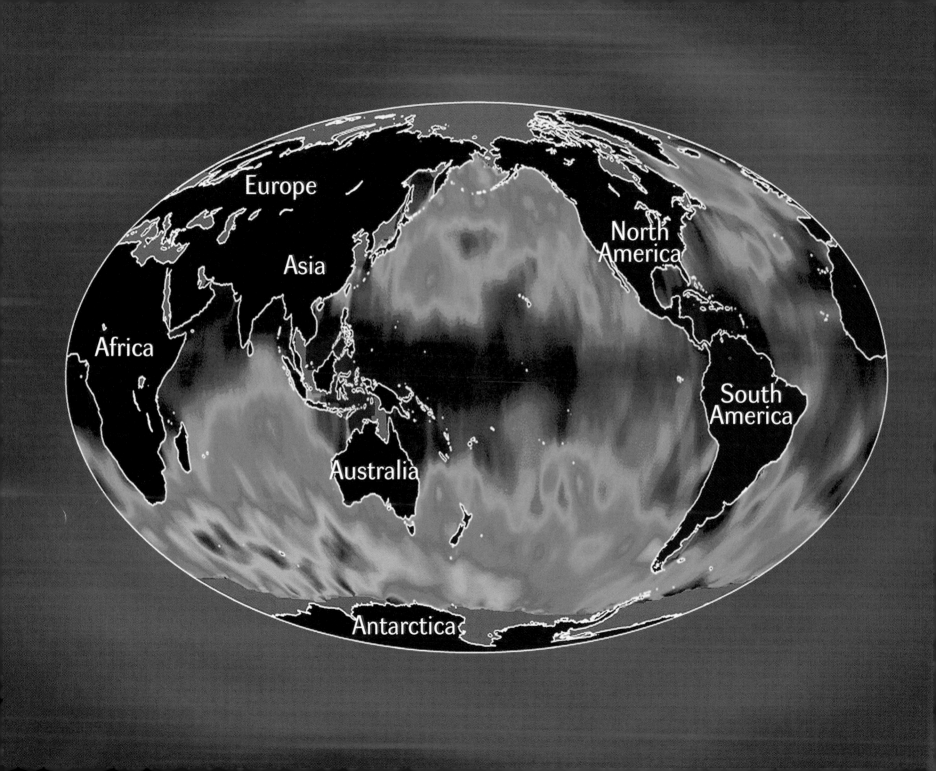

Look at the Oceans

Look at the map of the world on page four. Compare the amount of land you see to the amount of ocean. Is there more of one than the other? As you can see, Earth is covered mostly by ocean, not land. The ocean floor has mountains and valleys just like the **continents** do. Some parts of the ocean are very deep and cold. Other parts are shallow and warm. The difference in the temperature of the water is what makes it flow and move. The water temperature in the oceans also affects the temperature of the air. If the water is warm, the air tends to be warm, too. As the water in the ocean moves, warm and cold air move around Earth, affecting our weather.

The oceans are so big that you could spend your whole life studying them. For now, though, try out a few simple projects and see what you can learn!

This map of Earth was made on a computer. Scientists use maps like this one to tell how shallow or deep the oceans are, how their currents move, and other information about the oceans on Earth.

Watch Cold Water Sink

In the oceans, water temperature affects the movement of water. Cold water is heavy and warm water is light. When warm and cold water mix in the oceans, the cold water sinks to the bottom and pushes the warmer water out of the way. You can see how this works at home with a little homemade salt water and food coloring.

You will need

- A 64-ounce (2-l) glass jar, cleaned of labels (An empty juice container or pickle jar works well. A large glass bowl will work, too.)
- 8 cups (2 l) warm water
- ⅓ cup (78 ml) salt
- Blue food coloring
- Measuring cup
- Spoon
- Mixing bowl
- A paper cup
- A pencil or pen with a point
- A freezer

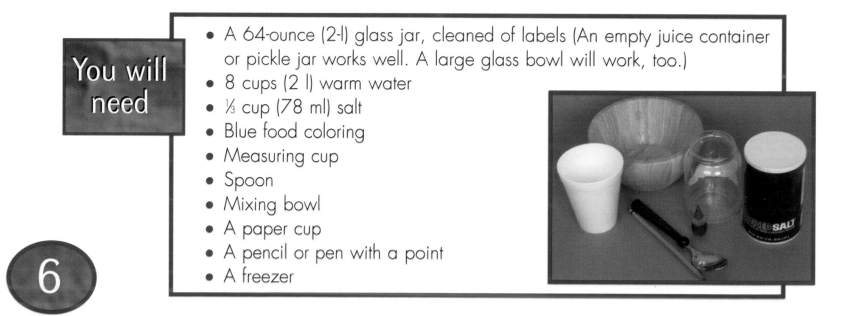

Add ⅓ cup (78 ml) of salt to 6 cups (1.4 l) of warm water. Stir until all the salt is dissolved. Stick your finger in and take a taste. This is about the amount of salt in ocean water.

 Measure 1 cup (237 ml) of the salt water and pour it into the mixing bowl. Add drops of blue food coloring until the water is dark blue. Put the bowl in the freezer until the water is cold.

 Pour the remaining warm water into a large, glass jar. Use a pencil to poke a hole in the bottom of the paper cup and rest the cup on the rim of the jar. The bottom of the cup should be underwater. (If you're using a bowl, someone will need to hold the cup over the water.)

 When the blue water in the freezer is good and cold, pour it very slowly into the cup and watch what happens. blue water will flow out and straight down to the bottom of the jar. Cold water sinks in the jar just like it does in the ocean!

Measure a Mini-Iceberg

Water moves in the oceans when cold water pushes warmer water out of the way. Most of the cold water in the oceans comes from the Atlantic Ocean near the North Pole. Large chunks of snow and ice, called glaciers, melt during the summer. Sometimes pieces of glaciers break off and float away. These are called **icebergs**. Icebergs float because ice is lighter than water, but most of an iceberg sits below the surface of the water. As it melts, cold water sinks to the bottom and makes the water around it move. You can make a mini-iceberg and watch it float and melt.

You will need

- 1 gallon (3.8 l) size zip-seal plastic bag
- A ruler
- A freezer
- A bathtub or sink
- Water

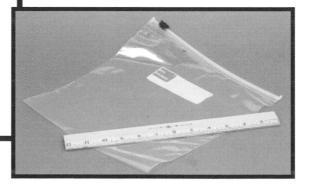

Fill up about half of the plastic bag with water and seal it. Place the bag in the freezer until the water is frozen.

 Fill a bathtub or sink with water.

 Take the chunk of ice out of the plastic bag. This is your mini-iceberg. Place the ice in the bathtub or sink.

 How much of the ice is underwater? Use a ruler to measure how much is underwater and how much is above the water. Ice is less heavy than water, so it floats.

Test Freezing Rates

During the winter in the North and South Poles, ocean water gets so cold that it often freezes at the surface. This creates large sheets of floating ice, called pack ice. Many animals sleep, hunt, and make their homes on pack ice.

If you live near the ocean, you may notice that it takes oceans longer to freeze than it does ponds or lakes. This is because the water in the oceans contains salt. The salt lowers the **freezing point** of the water. You can do an easy experiment to test the freezing point of salt water.

You will need

- Two 16-ounce (473-ml) plastic soda bottles
- 1 teaspoon (5 ml) of salt
- ⅔ cup (159 ml) water
- A cup
- A spoon
- A permanent pen
- A freezer
- Paper
- Tape

1 Label one bottle "freshwater" and the other bottle "salt water."

 2 Add 1 teaspoon (5 ml) of salt to ⅓ cup (78 ml) water and stir until it's dissolved. This is your salt water. Stick your finger in and taste the water.

 3 Pour the salt water into the bottle labeled "salt water." Pour ⅓ cup (78 ml) of water into the bottle labeled "freshwater."

 4 Place both bottles in the freezer and leave them there for half an hour. When you return, is one more frozen than the other? If neither is frozen, put both bottles back in the freezer and check again in 15 minutes. You should see that the salt water takes longer to freeze than the freshwater.

See How Waves Work

Wind creates **waves** when it blows across the surface of the ocean. Each wave of water has its own shape. If you look at an object floating on the water, you can see the shape of the wave. Waves have high points, called **crests**, and low points, called **troughs**. Objects floating on the water bob up as they go over a crest of a wave. Objects dip down as they pass through a trough of a wave. When the waves hit something, like a dock or beach, the pattern of the waves is broken and objects on the surface get thrown in many different directions. You can see how waves work with this simple experiment.

You will need
- A bathtub or a sink full of water
- A plastic bottle cap or a cork
- A spoon

1 Once the bathtub or sink is full of water, turn off the water and wait for it to settle. Gently place the bottle cap on top of the water in the middle of the bathtub or sink.

 2 Near one end of the tub or sink, use a spoon to slap the surface of the water. Watch the bottle cap. Which way does it move? Does it move up and down? Or does it move from side to side? It should move up and down as it travels on the crests and troughs of the wave. Don't make too many waves or you won't see them well.

 3 Remove the bottle cap from the tub or sink and wait for the water to settle. When there are no more waves, place the bottle cap in the water next to the side of the tub or sink.

 4 Slap the surface of the water again to make waves. What happens to the bottle cap this time? As the waves near the edge of the tub or sink, they get broken up, just like waves hitting a dock or steep shoreline.

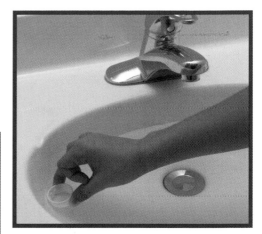

Study the Tides

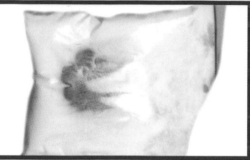

In most places where the ocean meets the land, the water level rises and falls on the beach. Sometimes the waves cover all the sand on the beach, and other times they stop far offshore. We call these changes in water level on land **tides**. Tides are caused by the pull of the Moon's **gravity**. When the Moon is closest to one side of Earth, it pulls the water toward it and causes a high tide. As the Moon moves away from that side of Earth, the pull of gravity lessens and the water flows farther out to sea. This is called a low tide. You can make a model of Earth, the Moon, and the oceans to study the tides.

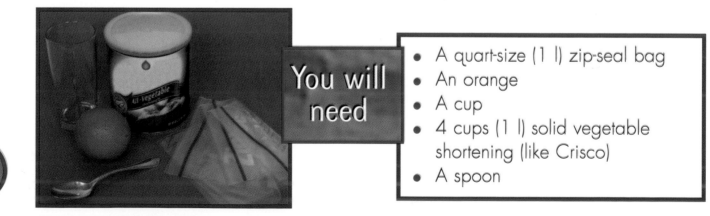

You will need

- A quart-size (1 l) zip-seal bag
- An orange
- A cup
- 4 cups (1 l) solid vegetable shortening (like Crisco)
- A spoon

Fill the zip-seal bag about ¾ full of vegetable shortening. In this project, the shortening is going to represent the water in the ocean.

 Place the orange in the bag. Move it around so it's covered in shortening. Seal the bag closed. The orange represents Earth.

 Set the orange on the rim of a cup and pretend you are the Moon. Which direction would the water in Earth's oceans be pulled?

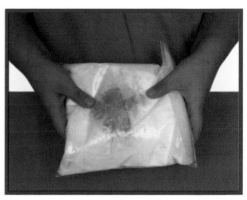

 Mold the bag so that the "water" is pulled toward you, the Moon. You should have bulges of vegetable shortening closest to you. Earth stays the same shape. If you change position, what happens to the "water"?

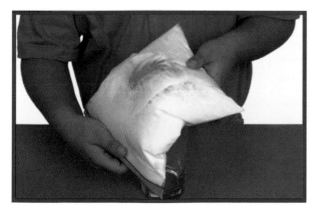

Make a Pen-Cap Submarine

If you ever went swimming and dove deep under the water, you might have felt a pain in your ears. This pain is caused by **water pressure**. The deeper you go underwater, the more water there is pushing down on your body and the more pressure you feel. Our ears hurt underwater because the water pressure squeezes the air in our ears and causes pain.

Submarines are ships designed to dive underwater. They use open spaces to control whether or not the ship sinks or floats. To float, the submarine forces air into its open spaces. To sink, the spaces are allowed to fill up with water. You can see how a submarine works with this project.

You will need

- An empty, clean, 1-liter plastic soda bottle and cap
- A pen cap with a clip attached (like the one shown)
- Clay
- Water

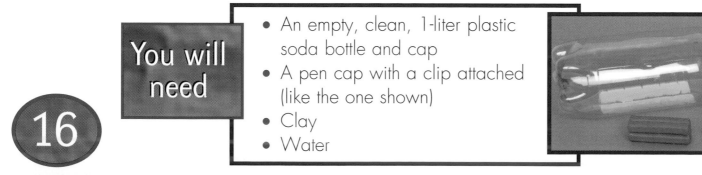

1 Roll a small, pea-size piece of clay into a ball and stick it on the clip end of the pen cap as shown. Fill the soda bottle half full with water.

 2 Slowly place the pen cap in the bottle, clay-end first. Some water will come out. The pen cap should float just beneath the surface of the water. If it sinks to the bottom, remove some clay and try again. If it won't sink below the surface, add a little clay to make a larger ball and try again. There should be a little bit of air trapped in the top of the pen cap.

 3 Make sure the bottle is half full with water and screw the top on the bottle tightly.

 4 Squeeze the bottle. What happens to the pen cap? Squeezing the bottle makes the air in the pen cap squish into a smaller space and lets in more water. This makes the pen cap heavy and it sinks. When you release the pressure, the air expands and the water drains out. This makes the pen cap rise. Submarines work in a similar way.

Create a Nautical Chart

The bottom of the ocean is very bumpy. Some places have deep **trenches**. Others have mountains that rise up near the surface of the water. The depth of the water is the distance from the surface of the ocean to the seafloor. **Nautical charts** are special maps that show the depth of the water in different places. One of the oldest methods of making a nautical chart involved stretching long cables to the seafloor and then measuring them. The length of the cable was the depth of the water. You can see how this method worked with this experiment.

You will need

- A shoebox with a lid
- Enough clay to cover the bottom of your shoebox, plus extra
- A pair of scissors
- A pencil
- A ruler
- A permanent pen
- Tape

1 Press a layer of clay into the bottom of the shoebox. Now mold the clay into large mountains and trenches. Try to make it look like land, with lots of hills and changes. This will be the bottom of your "ocean."

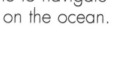

 2 Using a pencil with a sharp point, poke about 20 holes in the lid of the shoebox. If you need to, you can use the scissors to punch the holes. Try to make the holes small. Put the lid on the box and tape it down.

 3 Stick your pencil in one hole, point first, until it reaches the bottom. Draw a line on the pencil where the lid is. Now pull out the pencil and measure the length from the point of the pencil to the line. Write this number in pen on the box by the hole. This is the depth of your "ocean" at this point.

 4 Measure the depths at all the other holes in the lid and write them on the box. Sailors use maps like this one to navigate on the ocean.

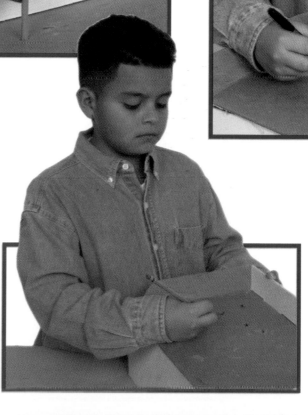

Watch Hydrothermal Vents Form

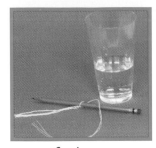

Hydrothermal vents are places on the bottom of the ocean that are formed when water seeps into the ocean floor and is heated by **magma**. The hot water melts some of the rocks underground and the chemicals from the rocks get into the water. When the hot water from underground reaches the cold water in the ocean, it cools off. As the water cools, the chemicals in the water **precipitate**, or fall out. These chemicals build up around the vents as tall, black **chimneys**. With this project, you can watch sugar dissolve in hot water and then precipitate in cold water.

You will need

- A large glass jar or drinking glass
- A piece of cotton string at least 8 inches (20 cm) long
- A pencil
- A paper clip
- 1 cup (237 ml) water
- Four cups (1 l) sugar
- A pot
- A spoon
- An adult

Tie the piece of string to the middle of the pencil. Attach the paper clip to the loose end of the string.

 Get the string wet and roll it in sugar. Now lay the pencil over the glass so the string hangs inside and the paper clip touches the bottom.

 Ask an adult to help you boil the water in a pot. Add 2 cups (0.5 l) of sugar and stir. The hot temperature of the water will help the sugar dissolve. The same thing happens at a hydrothermal vent. As water is heated by Earth, more things are able to dissolve in the water. Bring the water to a boil again and keep adding sugar until it starts collecting on the bottom of the pot.

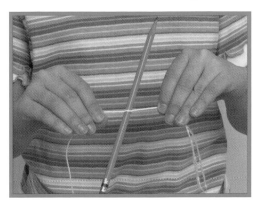

Pour the sugar water into the glass and wait. In a few hours or a few days, you'll start to see sugar sticking to the string. As the water cools, it can't hold as much sugar so crystals stick to the string. This is what happens when hot water from deep sea vents meets the cold ocean.

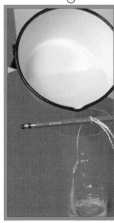

To Learn More

If you want to learn more about the oceans, there are a lot of places you can look. The best thing to do is to visit an ocean if you live near one. Taste the salty water, watch the tides, and look for shells on the beach. If you don't live near the ocean, find out if there's an aquarium near you. Aquariums are great places to learn about the science of the oceans.

From home or school, you can find many books and Web sites about the oceans. Ask your teacher to help you locate good information or try some of the Web sites recommended at the back of this book. If you wanted to, you could spend the rest of your life studying our oceans!

Glossary

chimneys (CHIM-neez) Tubes through which the water from hydrothermal vents flows.

continents (KON-tin-ents) The seven great masses of land on Earth.

crests (KRESTS) The high points of waves.

freezing point (FREEZ-ing POYNT) The temperature at which something freezes.

gravity (GRA-vih-tee) A force that attracts one object to another.

hydrothermal vents (hy-druh-THER-muhl VENTS) Places on the bottom of the ocean where hot water mixed with chemicals flows out.

icebergs (YS-bergz) Chunks of glaciers that break off and float away.

magma (MAG-muh) Hot liquid minerals inside Earth.

nautical charts (NAW-tih-kul CHARTS) Special maps that show the depth of the water in different places.

precipitate (preh-SIH-pih-tayt) To fall out.

submarines (SUB-muh-reenz) Ships designed to dive under water.

tides (TYDZ) The rising and falling of water on the beach.

trenches (TRENCH-ez) Deep holes in the ocean floor.

troughs (TROFS) The low points of waves.

water pressure (WAH-ter PREH-shur) When under water, water pressure is the weight of the water above you pressing down on your body.

waves (WAYVS) Patterns of movement.

23

Index

Web Sites

Due to the changing nature of Internet links, PowerKids Press has developed an online list of Web sites related to the subject of this book. This site is updated regularly. Please use this link to access the list: www.powerkidslinks.com/gesp/hopaoce/